Children

Catalogue for Exhibit of Art and Illustration by

Donna White-Davis

For collections, consignment, and exhibition

Table of Context

Artist's Statement

My art has been often termed as "Impressionistic" or the modern term given in Hyannis Port "Emotional Realism". I humbly accept each description. It seems that Art communicates emotion directly to the heart and soul. I know my inspirations come from scenes I may have glimpsed in a moment and saved forever in my heart and mind. Indeed once accepted the inspiration demands a painting. That is my fate. I offer it to you in hopes that the images will communicate with you and remain forever in your heart and soul.

Love, Donna

Inspiration

I had driven cross country photographing our beautiful country. It was 2001, fall, and the journey was incredibly healing. I began the journey in Martha's Vineyard and completed in California. I decided to add Washington DC and then coming home, camp for a while and photograph Asseteague MD where the wild horses run in the surf. I was weary and alone when I reached the campground. The people I found came there every September and welcomed me into their little group. As everywhere in America I travelled alone but found welcoming family. That night just after going to bed in my tent with the wild horses and deer grazing outside a new camper came in and pitched their tent. They were French and that night the father sang a loving lullaby to his 4 year old son who, in perfect pitch with the waves whisper on the shore, repeated the little song. I awoke at dawn as I always do when travelling to photograph. I walked the short distance to the beach to fill the sunrise. To my surprise, there below me on the beach sat the father and his little son waiting also for the new dawn.

That was the morning before the 911 tragedy and the beach faced North East in the direction of NYC. I drove home and awake the next morning to the 911 tragedy. I went to the camera and downloaded the sunrise of the day before. I had to paint the scene to heal. I never use projection of photographs in my art. I go to the spirit and paint from my store image, however to have the scene in both mediums give me a deep comfort.

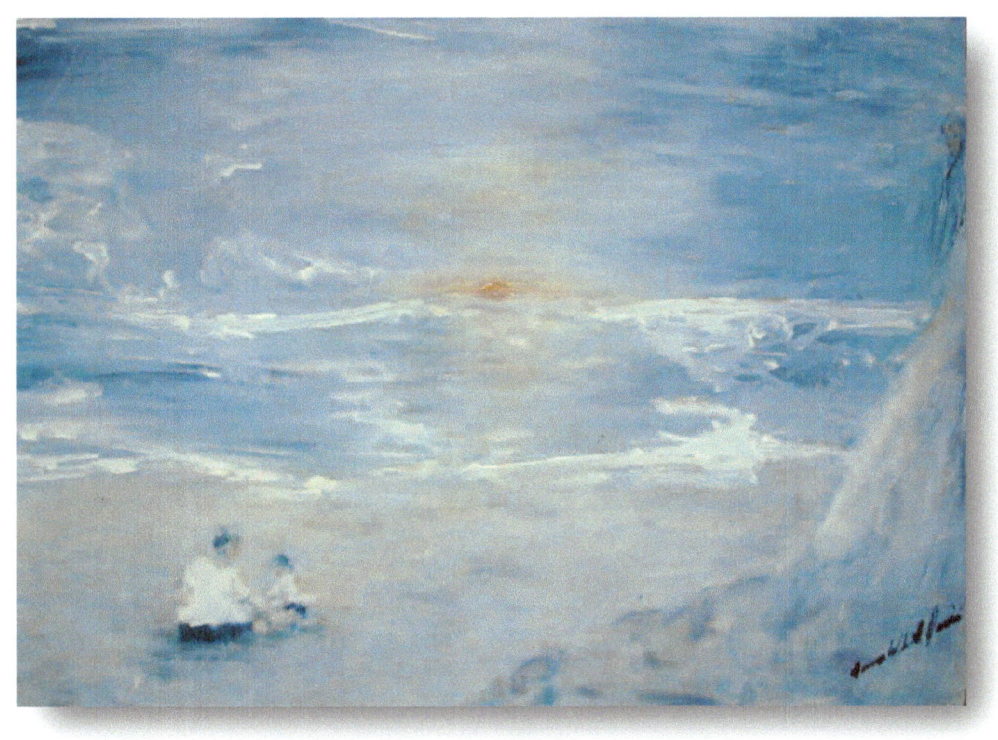

Asseteague Sunrise 19x25

Is there a time in life with greater emotion than creating, bearing and raising a child?   Peace Hearts I painted after hearing a peace worker say that he felt women were more peaceful because they slept with a baby heart beating under their heart for nine months. I thought of my pregnancies for my sons and remembered that is was my husband also who slept with our hearts.

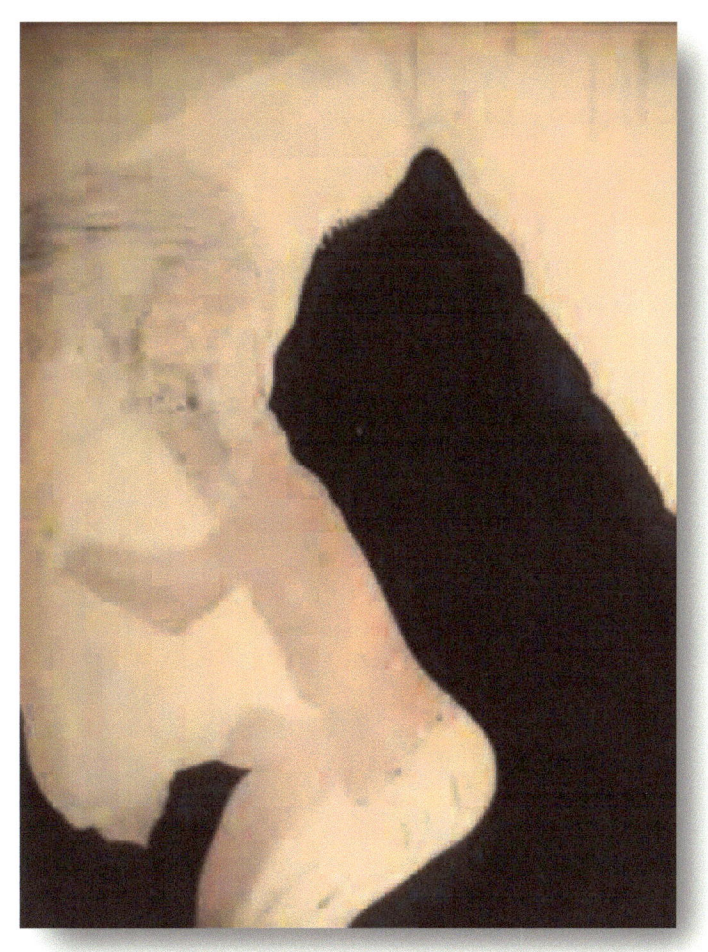

Peace Hearts 24x30

Memories of the farm are happy and very rich with warmth. I remember rising early in the morning in our bedroom where the winds gently blew fresh mountain air through the the flocked curtains as the birds began their morning sonnets I nursed the baby and planned the day.

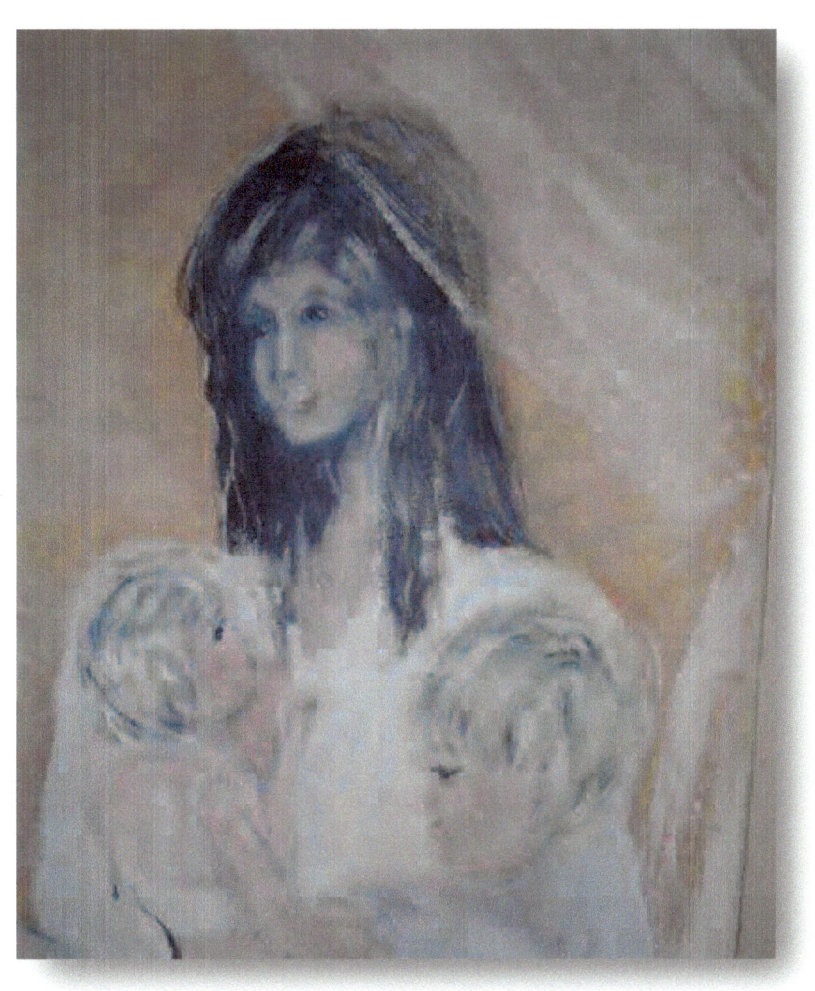

Esperance Dawn 28x38

I remember waking one evening in Esperance to find my husband talking with his new born son by the warmth of the kitchen stove. Winters were cozy as we moved our life from th large farm house to the smaller south side to conserve energy. The power often went out in the winter so those talks around the kitchen stove were always the best remembeed.

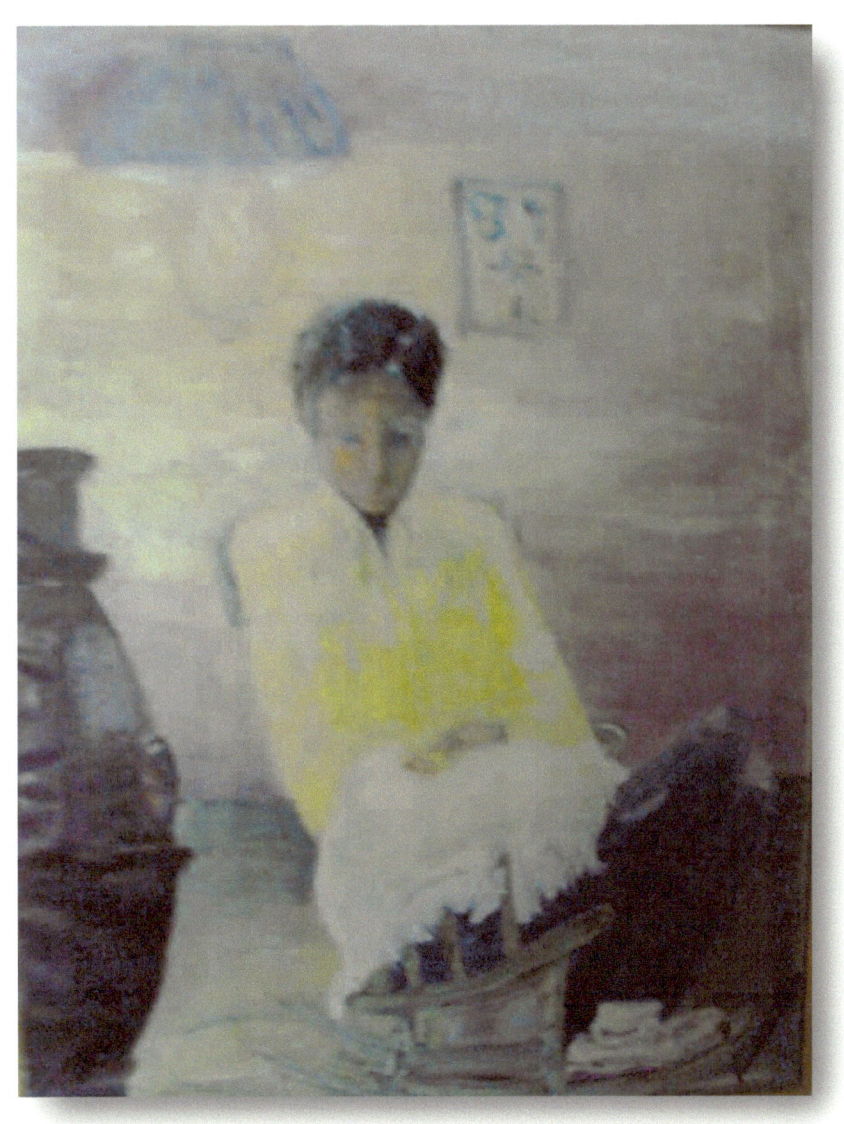

Esperance Evening 32x24

When I moved into the studio in the Catskills I was studying the paintings of Thomas Cole the founder of the Hudson river School and was pleased to find a painting that was commissioned for Cloe to paint a view of L'Esperance as Cole termed it. The painting depicts the artist overlooking the bridge in Esperance New York that also, to the north overlooked our farm. The man in my time who own that land was a Scotsman named Mr. Liddle who served as the town historian who often visited the children with stories of the way people lived at the time our 1874 farm was built. I painted this tongue in cheek copy placing our family on the hill overlooking our farm.

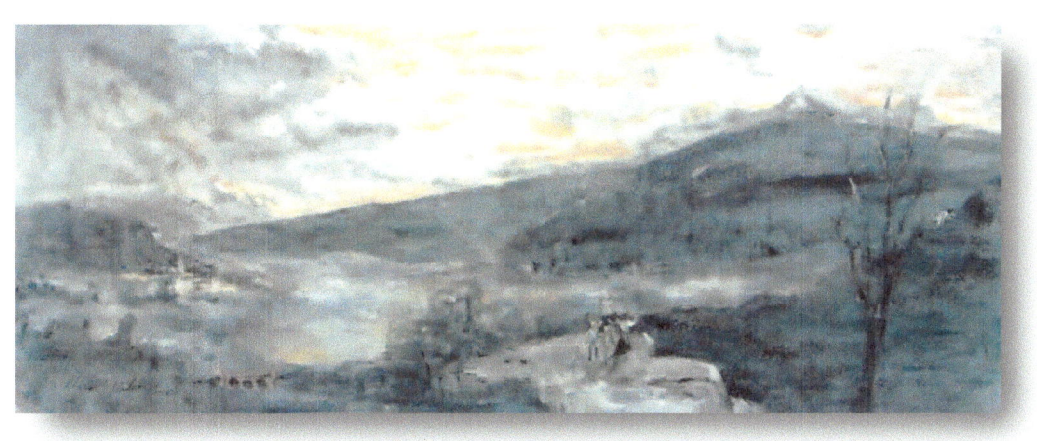

L,Esperance Good-Bye 28x15

We build an acre pond above the house because we had a slow feed well and needed the water. We brought in sand for the beach. I have a photograph of my eldest son stocking the frist Bass we stocked it with. All of the chilren in th evillage and indeed of my friends and colleagues in Albany came to swin those beautiful spring fed waters.

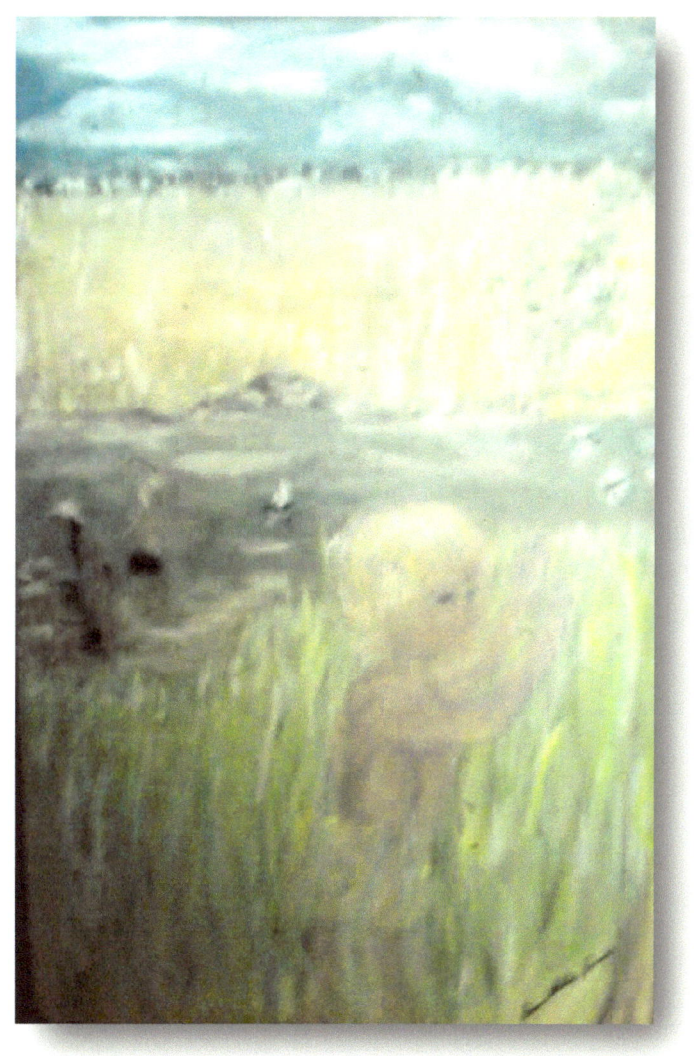

Esperance Summer -32 x36

This is a memory from my time living in Provence, France with my dear writer friends and their children. They were writing a hiking and eating book and we hiked the mountains of the Vergon gorge and found this village where thei son decided to sit under a Monet like tree. I have so many memories for that life I hope I have time in my life to paint.

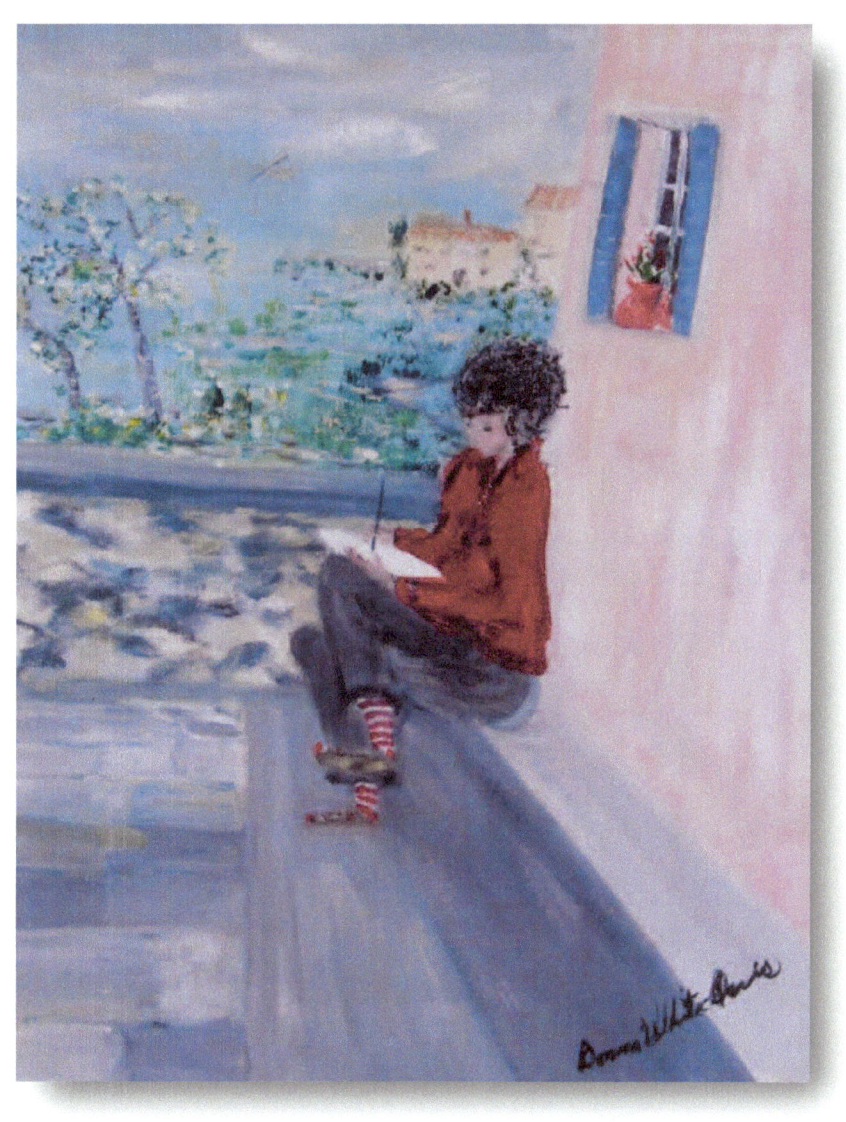

Le Jeune Artiste 15x19

I was inspired by a photograph in an album of a Woodstock friend of her baby daughter, a magical child of fantasy and imagination. Artist license was taken with the scene but the emotion of the child remains vivid.

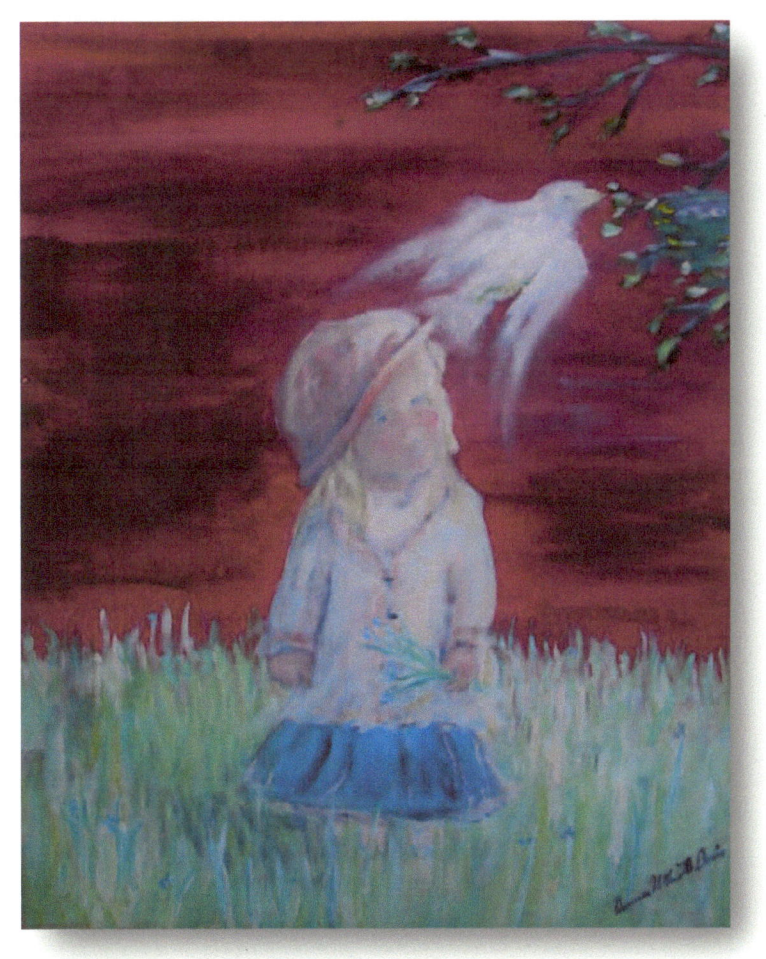

Dove at first sight 20x24

This painting actually belong with a series of mural paintings I created called Sermon on the Mount, the subject is obvious. It the exhibit I tried to represent those listening to Jesus's sermon giving us the words"Give us this Day our Daily Bread" as people from the world. From the same exhibit Sermon on the Mount

This painting was of Abraham, Sarah, and Isaac

Not only is it the unquestionably most comtempative of the Bilical stories

Abraham is seen as a forefother of Christian, Jews, and Muslim

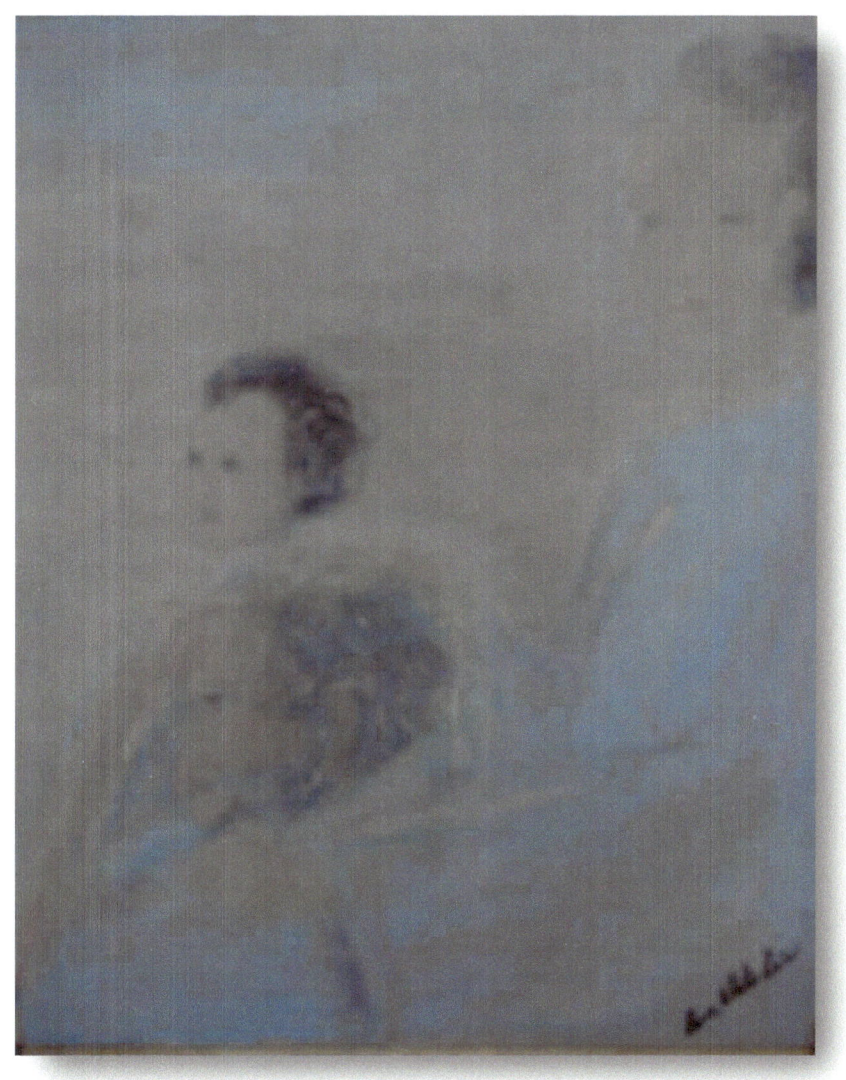

Abraham , Sarah, and Isaac 22x26

This is one of my favorite memories of Minnesota summers with my cousins, putting on plays swimming, fishing, and boating on the river. I'm the little one second from left.

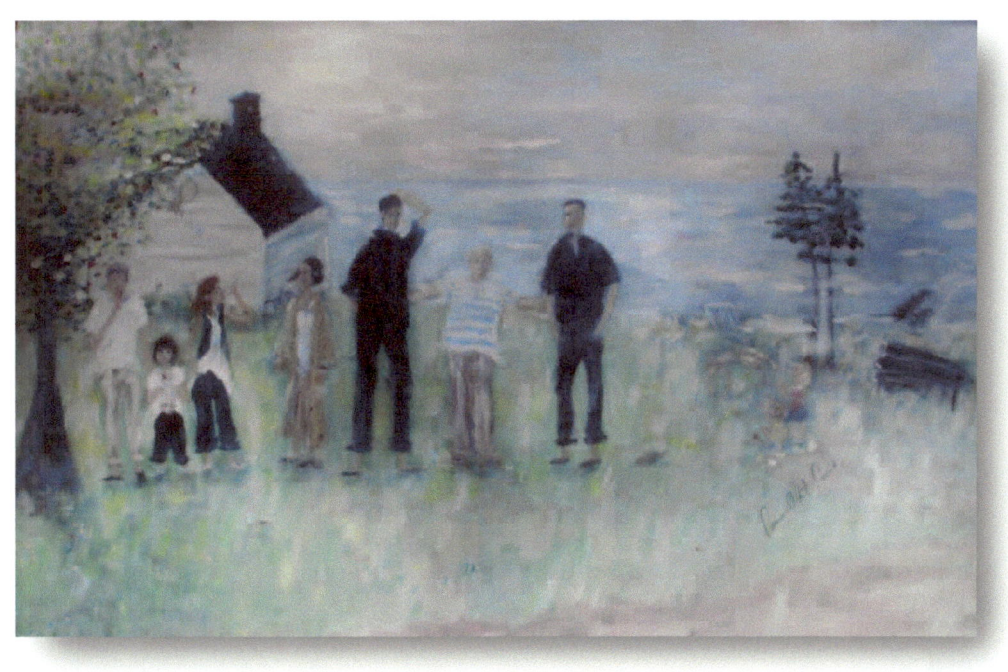

Minnesota Actors 1952 40x24

Private collections

The following paintings are in private or museum collection around the world

I retain th right to print from the originals

Framed prints, Giclee, posters and cards are availabe upon request

Family Portraits

I often am asked to painting my impressions of a family

and I offer commission arrangement for those patrons.

The following collections are available to Print as paintings, posters, and cards. All mountings are on museum quality , acid free paper and matting or framing is available.

Watercolors

Children and Families

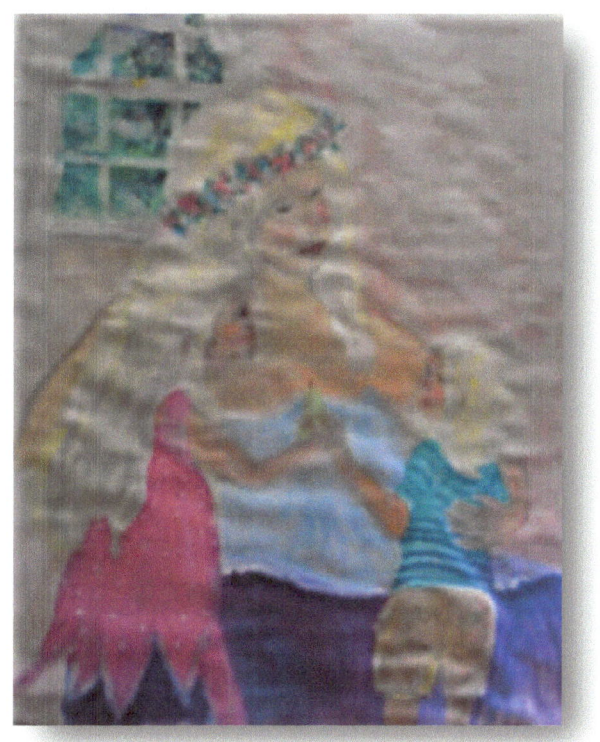

Paula

Canvass and Acrylic

Since I paint from primary colors and mix my own variations myself

the art has a beautiful nautural master essence

with very subtle gradients and a depth of image.

Colorado

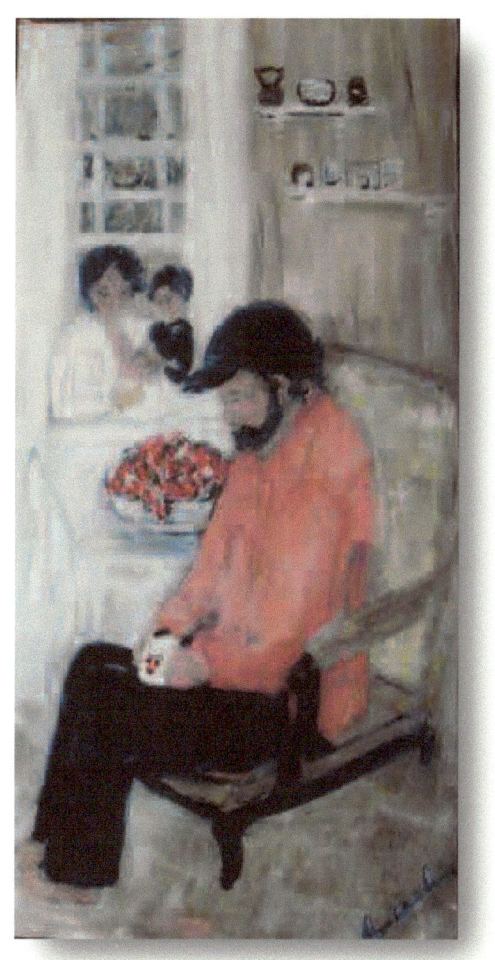

New Dad

The White House

Washington DC

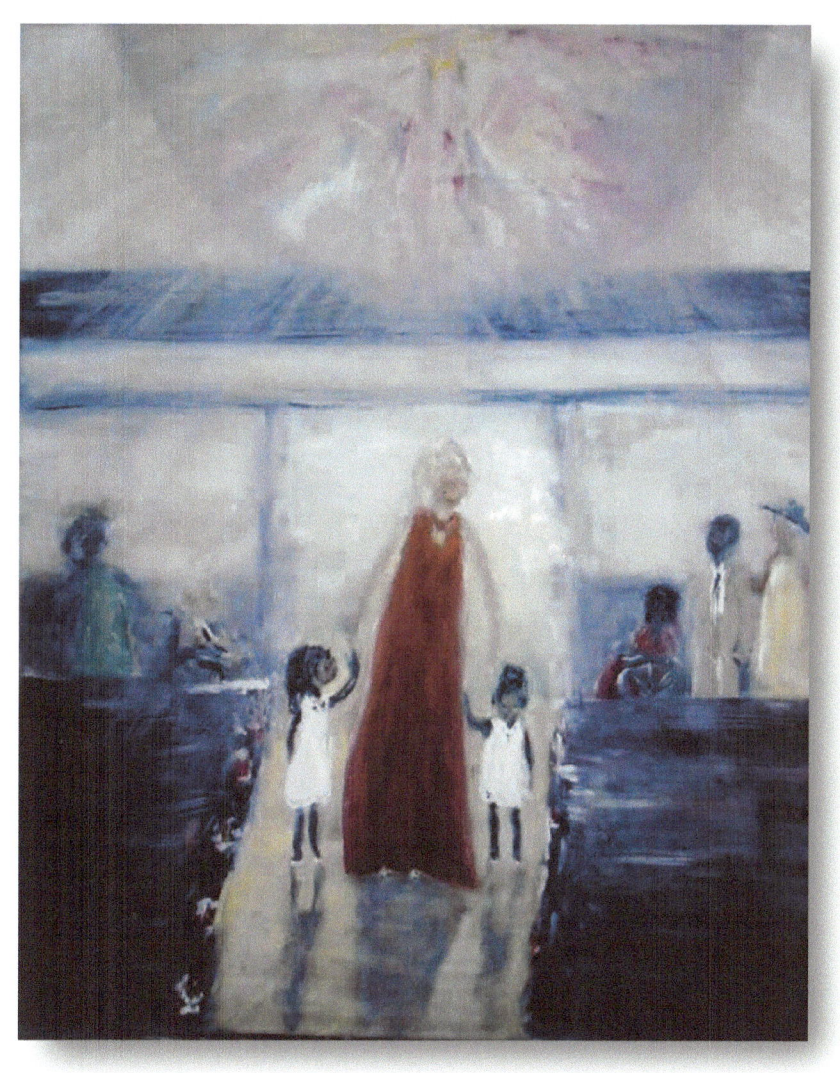

Rose Window Sisters

Congress

Washington, DC

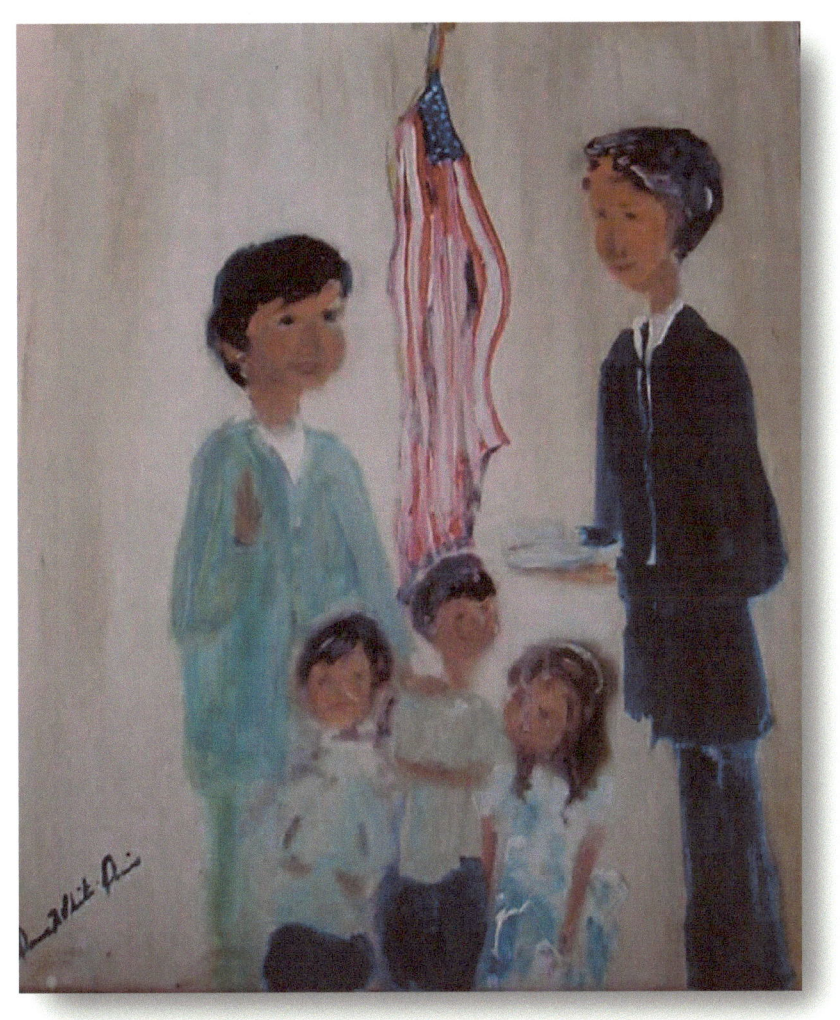

Grandma the Speaker of the House

New York Upstate

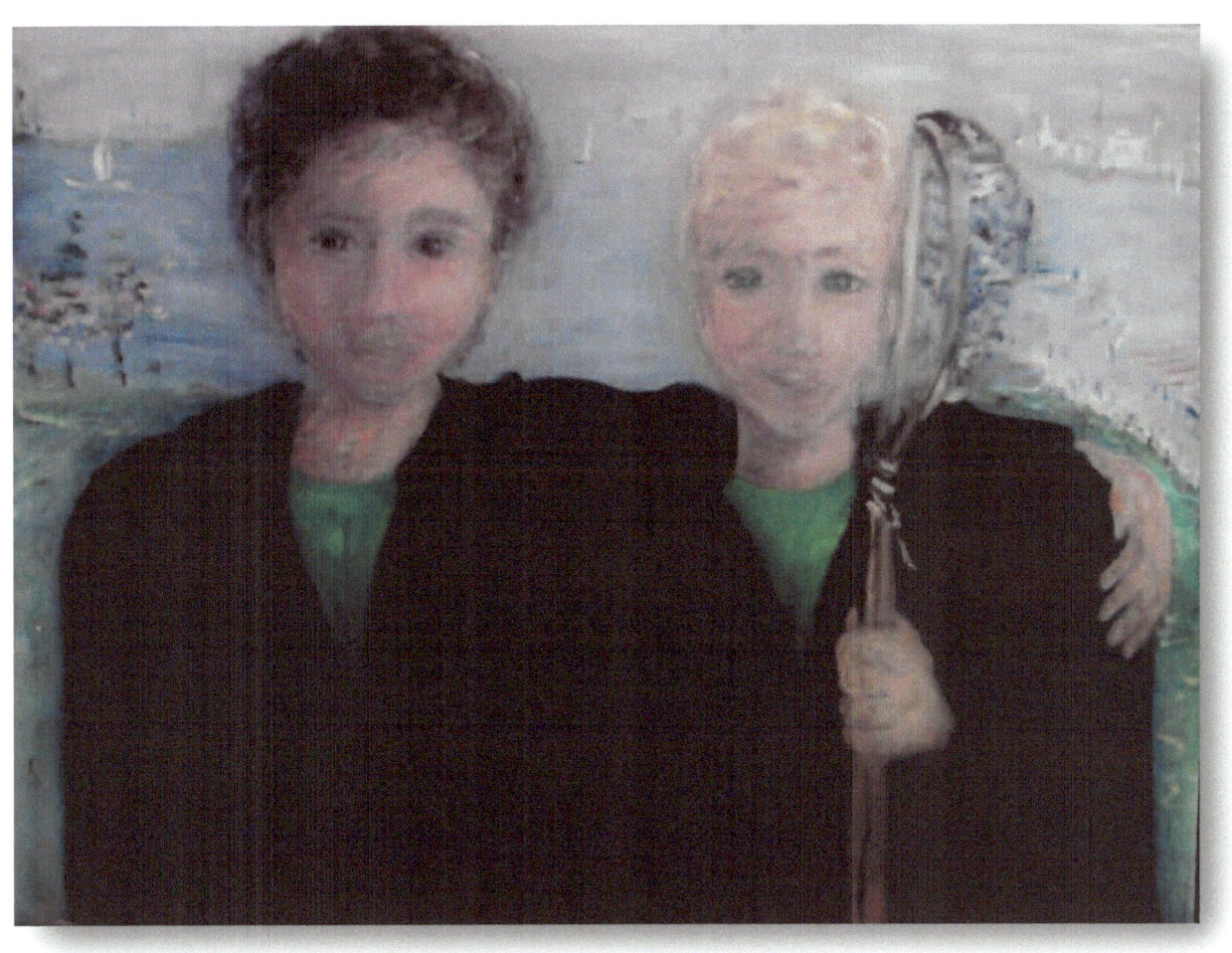

American Brothers. 1995

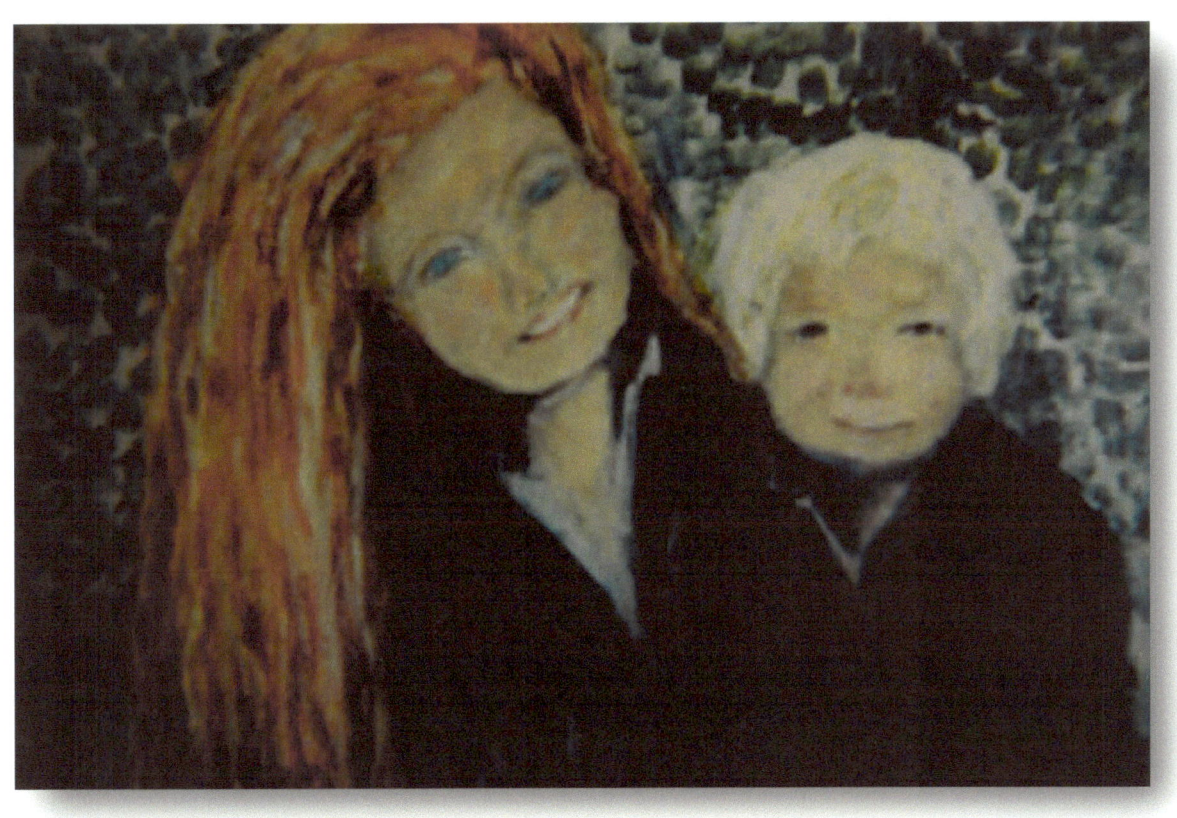

The Neighbor's Child

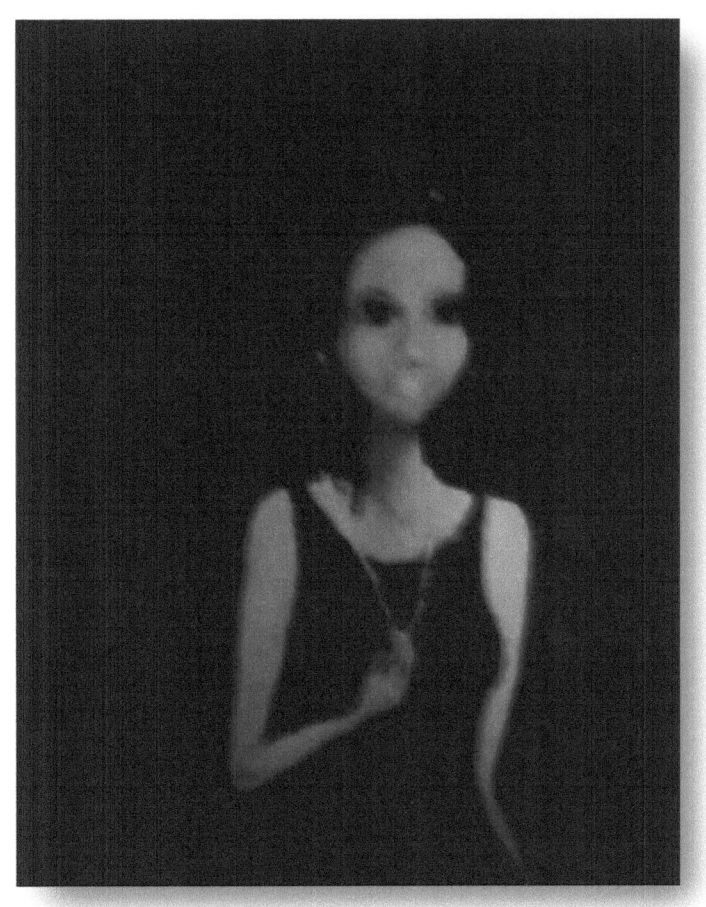

Prom Night

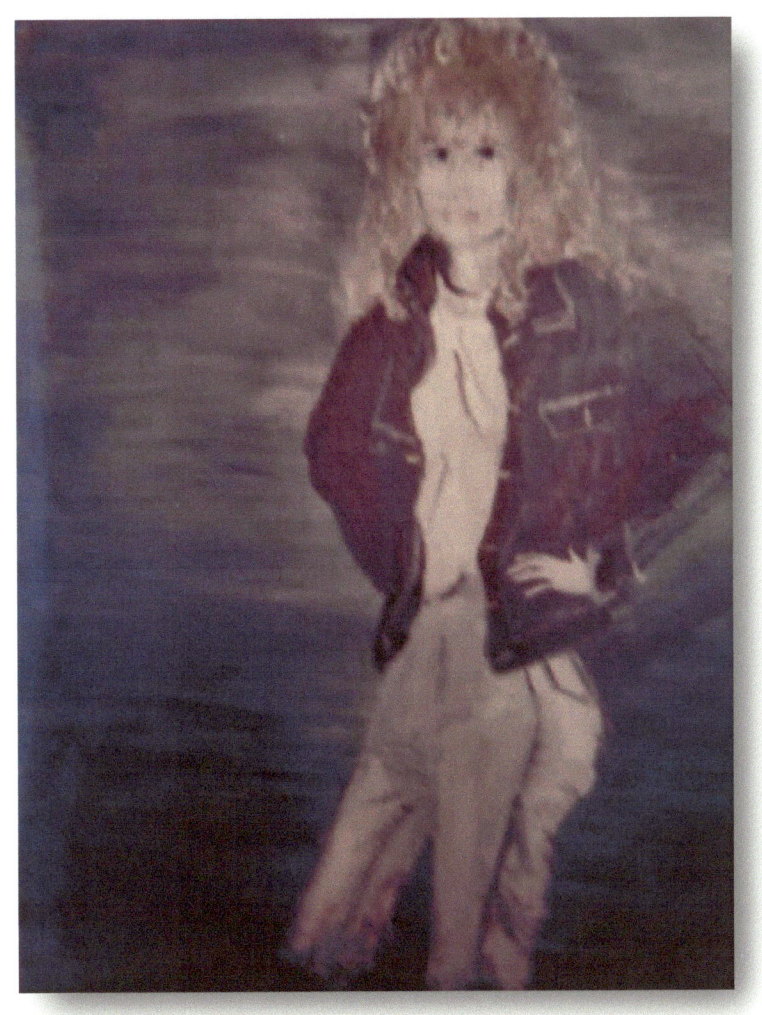

Nineties Nancy

New York City

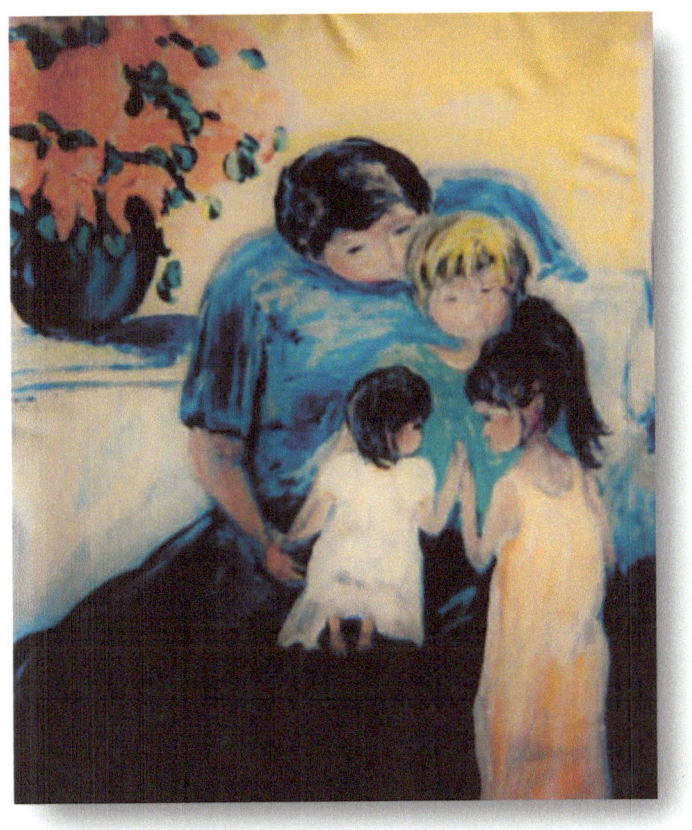

Katie's Gifts

England

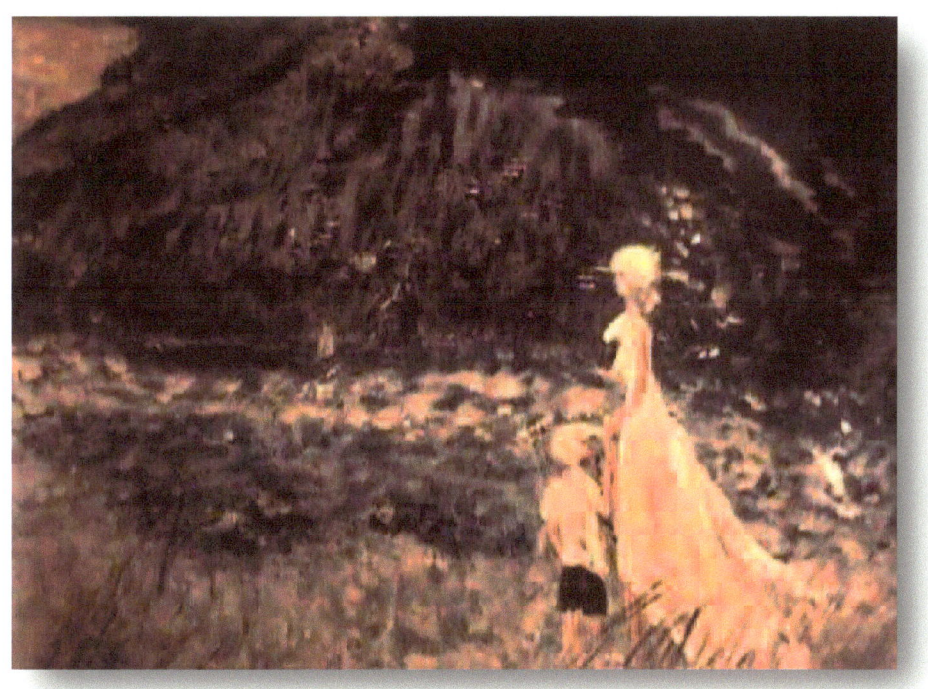

Diana

Hyannis Port

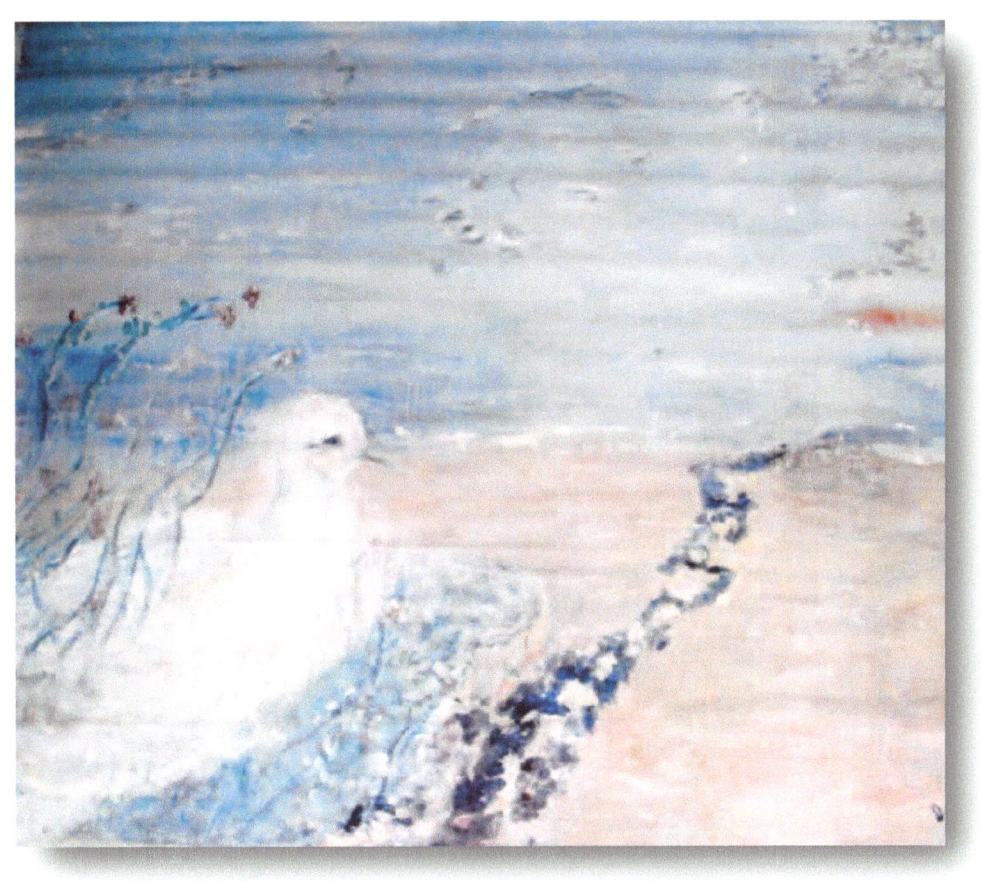

Ocean Beach Farewell

Watercolor Illustrations

Children

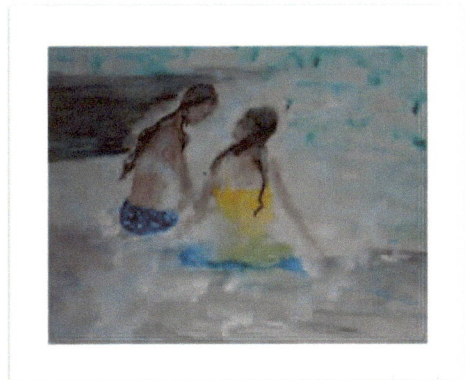

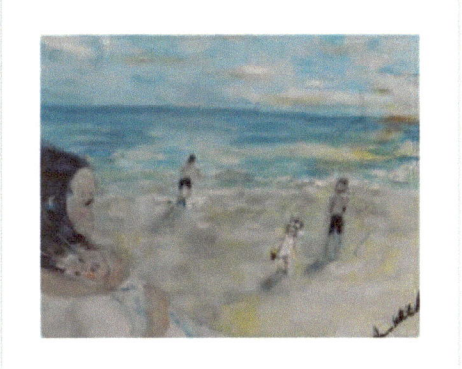

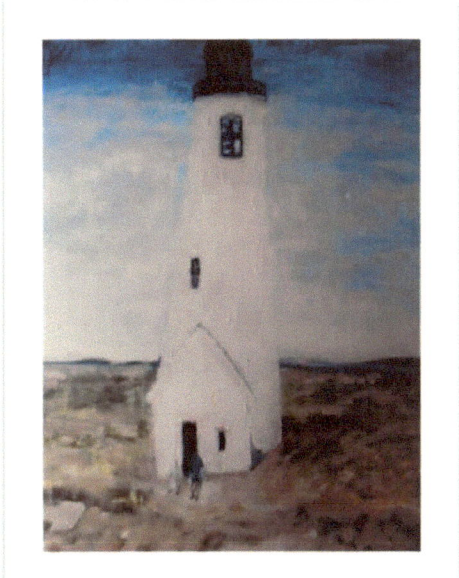

Canvass and Acrylic Illustrations

Since I paint from primary colors and mix my own variations myself

the art has a beautiful nautural master essence

with very subtle gradients and a depth of image.

Lillies

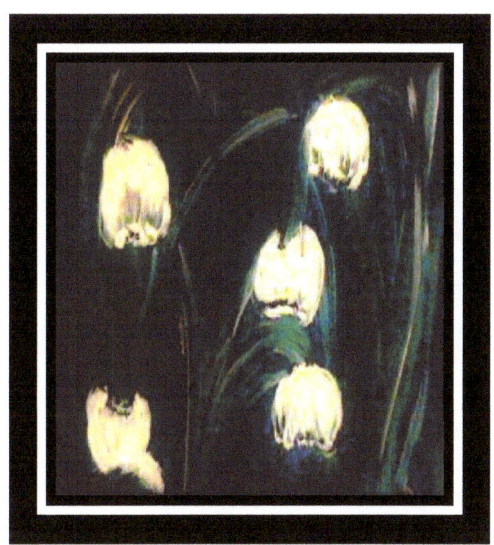

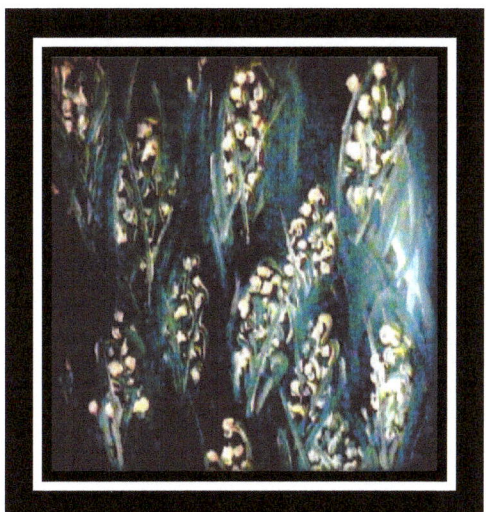

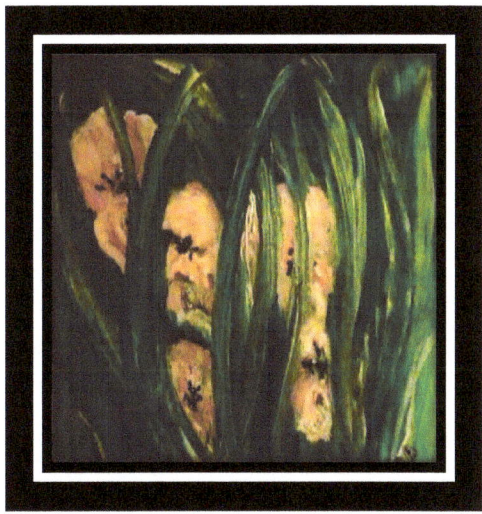

I had just attended and freelance photographed the first Woodstock Film Festival 1999

And decided to moved to the Catskills and study open seminars and presentations

at

the Center for Photography

At Woodstock

And the Woodstock School of Arts

I was driving to my new studio when this scene presented itself . I loved the balance, the care, the hard

working graderning dressed with the apron.

It was one of my first paintings form the Catskills.

I plan to do many.

Americana

Working

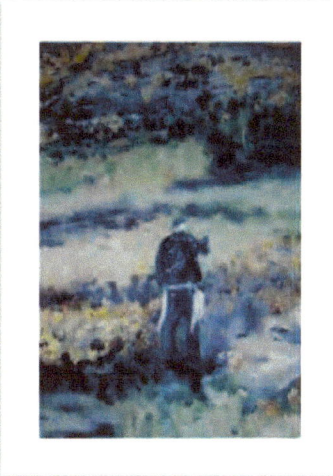

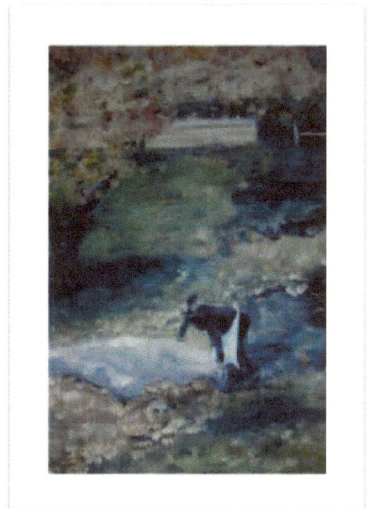

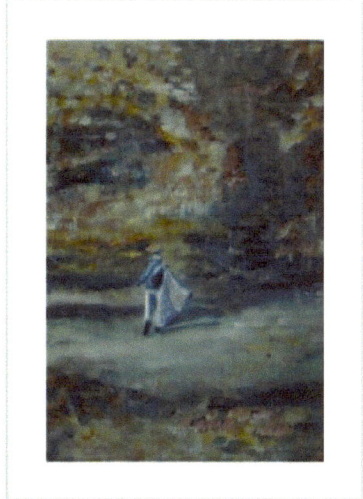

Previous Exhibitions

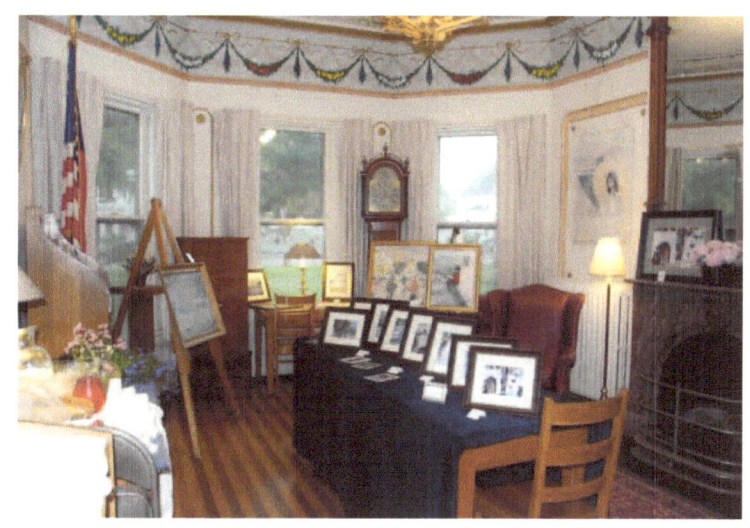

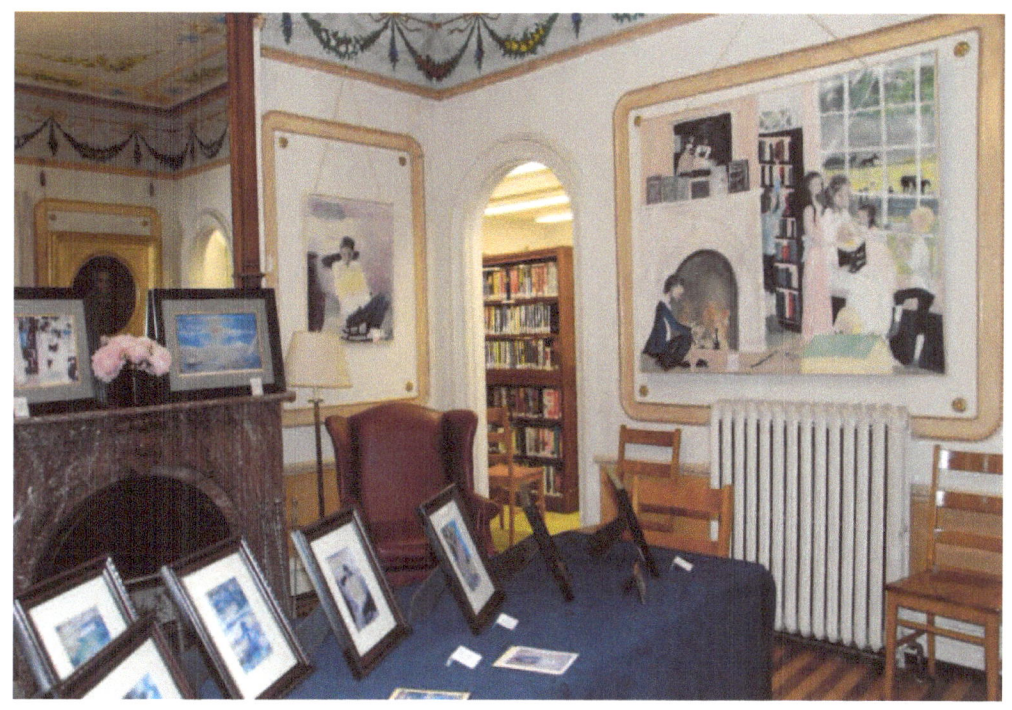

Catskill Library

Palenville Branch

Palenville New York

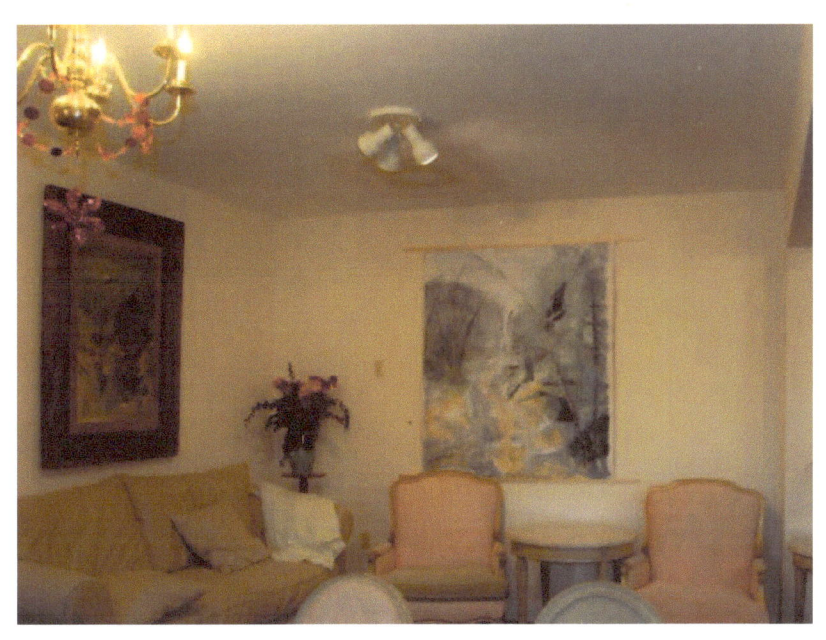

Photo Essay Exhibit

Colony Café

Woodstock, New York

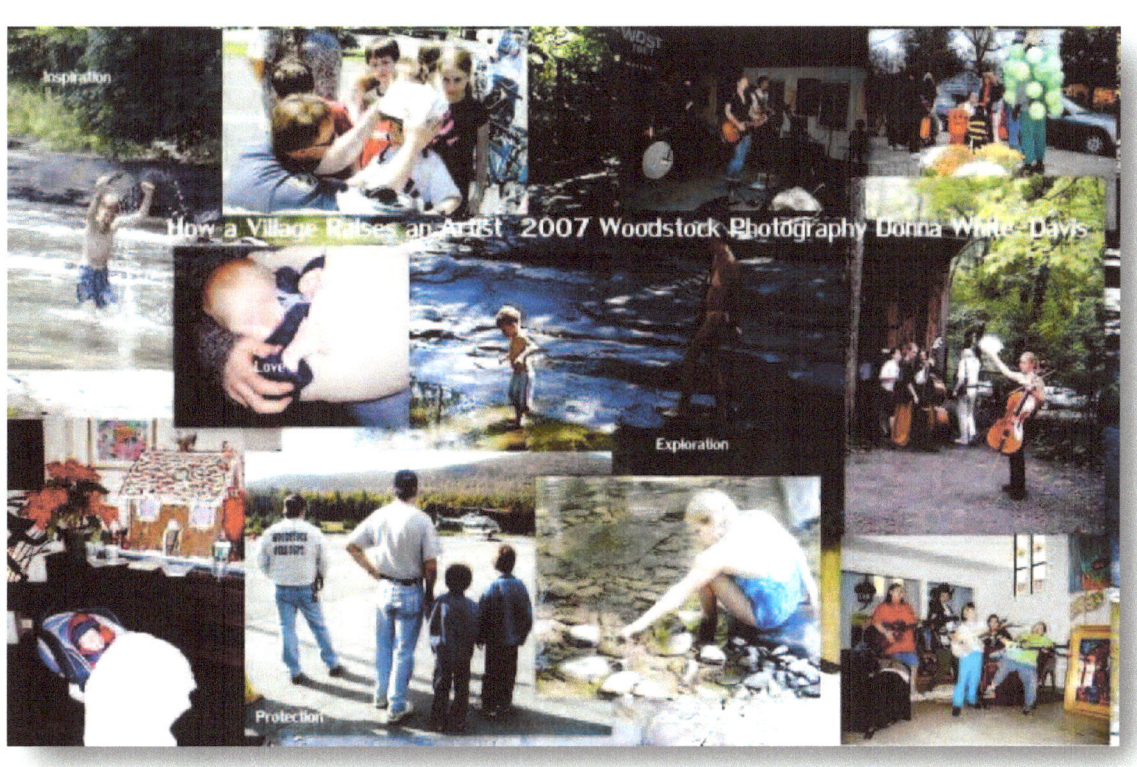

How a Village Raises an Artist   2007 Woodstock Photography Donna White-Davis

New Photo Essay book that speaks for itself

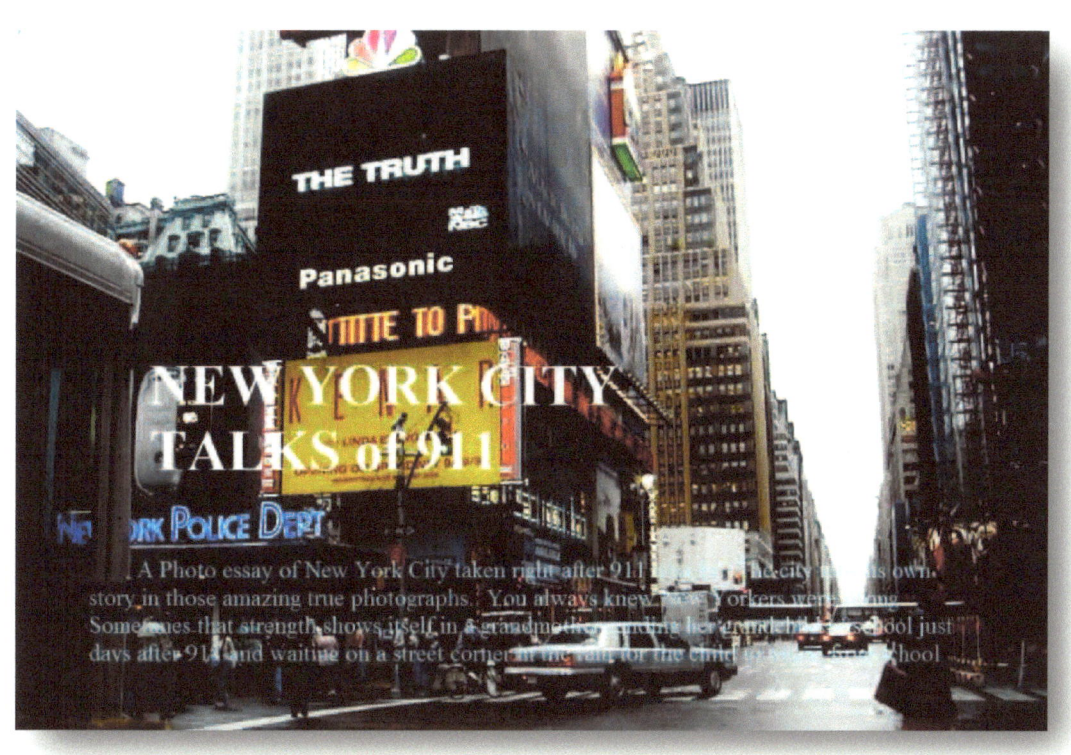

NEW YORK CITY
TALKS of 911

A Photo essay of New York City taken right after 911. The city tells its own story in those amazing true photographs. You always knew New Yorkers were strong. Sometimes that strength shows itself in a grandmother taking her grandchild to school just days after 911 and waiting on a street corner in the rain for the child to come out of school.

For

Originals, Consignments, copies

Contact

Donna White-Davis

P.O.Box758

Woodstock, New York 12498

donnawhitedavis@hotmail.com

845 901-5603